THE BODY SERVANT

THE BODY

SERVANT

Poems of Exile

JAMES KIRKUP

LONDON: J. M DENT & SONS LTD

First published 1971

© James Kirkup 1971

Made in Great Britain
at the
Aldine Press · Letchworth · Herts
for
J. M. DENT & SONS LTD
Aldine House · Bedford Street · London

ISBN: 0 460 03847 8

In Memory of Morgan

ACKNOWLEDGMENTS

'Expoem' appeared in *Chunichi Shimbun, Poetry Nippon* and *Japan Quarterly*.

'Emily in Winter' appeared in *The New York Times, Poetry Australia* and *Workings*.

'Lost Soul' appeared in *The Poetry Review*.

'The Sacrifice' appeared in *Poetry Australia*.

'In Memoriam: Bertrand Russell' appeared in *Eigoseinen*.

'Shoji' appeared in *Poetry Nippon*.

'Visiting the Graves in Zoshigaya Cemetery' appeared in *The Japan Times Weekly*.

'Toki' appeared in *The Times*.

vii

I know a noble guest   dear to princes
whom grim hunger   cannot harm
nor hot thirst   nor age nor illness.
If kindly the servant   always tend him
he who must go   along on the journey
safe and certain   they will find at home
food and joy   and countless kin
but sorrow if the servant   obeys his lord badly
his master on their journey;   nor will brother fear brother
when unharmed they leave quickly   the bosom of their kin
mother and sister.   Let whoever will
with fitting words   name the guest or the servant
I speak of here.

(Anglo-Saxon riddle)

[Answer: Soul and Body. The guest is the soul; the servant, and
brother, the body.]

CONTENTS

ix

ECONOMIC ANIMAL FARM

HEART MURMURS

THE LITTLE TREATISE OF ANATOMY

'. . . the neck bone's connected to the knee bone . . .'

HANDS

Fingers kept on tempterhooks,
hands, always before our eyes
except when in guessinggames
we hold them behind our backs—
these two fans of flowers,
black bone, gloves' pronated
gatherings, and flesh translucent
held to sunlight, lamplight,
adorned with rings on rings
of stone, wrinkles, metal, time,
knuckled with jewels, gold or silver,
above or under the skintight
gloves of flesh or gloves of kid—
petalled with ten pink nails,
mapped with the lines
of work and fate—these two
not dependent creatures move
and live and have their being—
crisping separately on
the grasped chords of keys
in common harmony or dissonance,
handling tools with ambidextrous grace,
panhandling man, manhandling pans,
penhandling pens, conveying
fruit, wafers, water, wine to
sightless mouth with only
occasional slips betwixt,
washing themselves intelligently,
all over, like a pair of cats,
playing with bats and balls,
counting notes and coins and cards,
neatly folding or hurriedly crumpling
cloth, paper, pastry—like birds
darting through books of leaves,
passing themselves through hair, over
the bloom of flesh on other flowers,
other lovers, apt at gratification of
the self and others, experts

3

at excitation, masturbation
and manipulation, they
can also soothe and cool and bless—
can be laid away quietly at night
like glove-stretchers, castoff skins
in drawers, behind doors, under floors
to sleep their own lightfingered dreams
far from the bodies they
bedewed and drugged and fumbled
with blood, sweat, tears and sperm—

And though they are always
making this compact with one another,
they can never quite bring off
their double harakiri, deaths
of samesex lovers, evermore united in
the nude handclasp of the sword.

After the last handshake,
hands gripping their own wrists,
one hand chops off the other
only to realize—always too late—
there is no brother now to give
le coup de grâce en un tour de main
or amputate him with a tightening
bracelet of cheesewire.

                        And then,
more solitary he, the lonely twin,
than anyone can ever know,
weeping with sad humiliation,
he must lay his final wrist upon
the throbbing rail of a coming train.

FEET

Gourd-shaped, slender soles
trimmed with tens of toes,
you do not move—no, it is
the ground that goes beneath you—
city streets, country lanes,
escalators, moving walkways,
mountain flanks, grassy fields,
plains of snow, deserts of dust.
Waters of lakes, rivers, seas
you walk upon or fan like fins.

You sense your way along
so many tightrope clews between
the place you want to go to
and the place you are told to go to,
from here and there
to everywhere, and go, man, go
heel-toe, heel-toe
in the dance of life
the dance of death
on the earth that moves you
step by step, step by step,
and crawls, shuffles, slopes,
runs, jumps, slides beneath you,
sending you, sending me
somewhere away and nowhere
else until we
trip—
        the earth no longer moves
and we are laid full-length
upon our shadows, and upon
those ghosts that live not only in Japan,
those ghosts that have no feet.

SHOULDERS

Swinging slightly from
side to side, or hunched
with good ideas like
a Buddha's in perpetual
immobility of meditation—
shrugged in bewilderment,
contempt, incomprehension, joy,
dropped in exhaustion, grief
or temporary disappointment,
clasped on the verge
of chilly British baths
by your own extensions,
arm-lifting hands, or
acrobatically raised
to rub an earlobe that
tickles when the arms are full;
rolled backwards, rolled forwards
in relaxed rotations,
clad in your own muscle
like ripe fruits or snowballs,
sprouting blades of angel-wings
or holding up the universe—

but most of all
most beautiful
when bearing
the heavy water-pitcher of Aquarius.

SKELETON

Creature dazzlingly white
within my scarlet cloak of blood,
you shimmer through my flesh
in X-ray attitudes or
funfair excruciations,

dislocations and contortions,
marrow-bright manifestations,
ectoplasmic ecstasies
in séances of skin
and radiances of screen.

Strung like a fractured doll,
limbs linked with invisible wires, from
the ceiling of a puppet-show,
spinal column segmented, just like
a toy snake's bamboo bits—
walking and reclining, standing
ever in my shadow,
shadow white in shadow black,
brilliant as radium or neon,
burning in the blackness
of my body in the night,
blazing in the brightness
of my body in the day—
beautifully bald,
exorbitant,
and ever masked by
that one revealing smile.

KNEES

Jointings of joy
that let me dance
or genuflect,
run up life's endless
stair, and down again,
or kneel in prayer
on hassock or on cobbles,
your heart-shaped caps,
carapace that cushions

all my falls from grace,
scarred with the fights,
kicks, crimes of childhood—
I behold your history
of hurts, obliterated now
by one head
laid tenderly upon my
double cobbles.

CHEST

Box, barrel, bastion
of the heart and lungs,
rigid with side-
winding ribs, yet
accordion-pleated,
bagpipes, bellows of bone
breathing like the sea
or panting like a storm
with love, hope, terror—
thorax pinked
with trim, self-centred
nipples, edged with armpits,
planted precisely at the pit
with one involuted navel.
(Two would look peculiar.)

HIPS

Sexy swivellers on ball
bearings, simply made
for the brackets of hands,
fringes of fingers,
the hoop of belts
or hula, hollowing
to fleet waist,

rich crupper, haired
to a point, and downed
with gold or black—
swung with abandon
in bottomless trances
or rippled by riverruns,
white stencil of skintight
trunks on sunblacked
bikini bareness—
briefly printed with
overleaning willowleaves
in the plunging fall
of a dewy diver's
chute des reins.

BUTTOCKS

Jolly bottom, witty rump,
in lax repose
or bouncing bump,
something to sit on,
beautiful bum,
lovely to lie on
in rain and sun—
a lowly beauty
elevated in
obeisance,
tall torso's stand
and counterpoise,
legs' capital
and furnishment,
pediment and pride
in perfect balancement—
my body's
heavenly hinge.

SPINE

Kite's knotted tail
hung aloft, dangled
on springy string,
controlled cascade
of rippling bone,
vertebrate inveterate,
dismembered column
re-articulated, snapped
pearls re-strung,
abacus of wired beads
with power to suspend its
self on nothing, like
a toppling but not top
heavy fountain—
made to curl itself
into a hoop
in death or sleep,
or to support untangled
(Indian rope-trick)
whole contraptions
of the head and face,
chatter and chew
of gnathic gnashings
on a single thread
life hangs by—
Allowing all newfangled
feet and ankles, knees
and legs to traction,
arms to swing, hands to strangle,
steps to wander, arms to handle—
connecting thread
between the earth and sky—
once snapped, thrown
within the grave alone
its bony dice must lie.

THIGHS

Thailand thighs!
Surf-riders,
striders in the long
boots of riverwaters,
ocean waves that
pull their pants up,
lake-lollings
gartering the groin.

Waders through snow
and grass and corn,
bathers in dew and dust,
the bevelled artificers
of leaping lust,
scissors
cutting the high
jump's
pole, rod or perch.
Frog meat.

HEAD

Bullet or ball
from gun, cannon
nodder or booted
by soccer great
or rugger tough
from pillar to
past is kicked
in thudding games
of pain and think,
nodder and shaker
of know and tell,
blinker and taster
of heart and hell—

11

the intellect is swell
behind the brows
but what can dwell
beyond the brain,
skullbox in the rain
of information, shrunk
to nothing but
a walnut,
wizened, or
a roast pea
nut?

Just think.

BREASTS

Lovely lollipops of life,
these pear-shaped pairs
or jellyfish jollywogs
justright or jaded—
ladies! have
a good bust!—
pointing to the stars, or
hanging in rags in a
starved child's mouth,
bounteous or only so-so,
doubly rich, implanted
with coarse rosettes,
pink buds, dark flowers
of milk and money, or
cut off with a canker's
vertical scar,
an Amazonian jest.

We make our choice in love
between the single-breasted girl,
the humble double-pearl, or
showy-breasted dove.

ELBOW

Dangle a basket,
haul a child,
cage a football,
link with another
or with two together.
Bend it and
watch that muscle.

Funnybone
electric nerve
the shock
of naked wires on
deadpan daggers
dig in the ribs
pointed remark
edging its way
through converse crowds
of nudging ambiguities—
erect on knee,
cupped in palm,
an open frame
of arms is formed
on which the chin
nestles a dimple
hinting at everything—
especially that.

Out at elbow,
more power to
akimbo kinks!
Come link with me!

FACE

It is where
I cannot see it
out of sight not
out of mind
can be explored
with hands, fingers,
pencil, tongue.
I can smell
my knee with it,
gaze in my navel,
bite my ankles like
a dog let loose upon
myself, or suck my toes.

I can hear
my heart with it
and taste a raindrop
putting out a long
pink feeler curved
like a hand to
see if it's stopped,
perverse pronation.

All wreathed around
a hidden smile I
feel only, rarely
see, except in
someone's eyes.

VULVA

Tenderly dismember me
in penal servitude, O
airy hairy-fairy, sans
teeth, with so much else—
or like a screaming
pink plastic zipper

vagina dentata
to catch by the cock
or nick the fretilla—
whirlpool, helical
nut for a proper screw,
a bathful of hot
soapy water sucking
my naked heel, my tool's
spinning top.

Sea-urchin split
or water-chestnut,
fresh with weed
and tressed with cresses—
a breathing clam,
aromatic, velvet-rough,
actively vegetable,
furred with vibrations,
wet clench of luck:
like nothing else—
a good fuck.

It never comes amiss.
And the next best,
a good piss.

ANUS

Dark star
in cheeks of cloud
or like a ripe
fruit in parted fronds,
brown berry,
cheerful cherry,
humble but not base,
with your own frank
country face,

forever chaste because
forever raped,
beyond virginity,
self-immolated,
excremental kiss
of pleasure-pain—
one wound that heals itself
with mere twists of sheer paper,
muscle that contracts
distensions, closes
like a sleeping eye
in one sly wink—
a mouth, politely
pouted on its eating,
like a poet's mind
veiling the secretions
hatching the creations
it must both stomach
and repulse.

Even in the best of circles,
an occasional belch
or netheructation
is to be condoned—
whether it whistles,
blares or shouts
falsettoes, fanfares,
folderols or merely,
as in any man of parts
(or woman too)
nobly farts—
or trumpets an involuntary
voluntary, though not a final
trump, we find its breath,
of the earth, earthy,
can instruct us in
the nice ecologies of our decay,
the origins of matter—
and our own
posthumous end.

16

PENIS

Members only!
Can be stiff
or still, stout
or slim, but
with his own
intelligence, in touch
with the brain's.
Dangles a purse
of shifting values
like the scales
of blind justice, racked
by vulva-envy, anus-angst.

However much our will
compels him, like
an admirably
independent spirit, he
acts when he feels like it,
often bestirring himself
without our permission,
and sometimes, indeed,
without our knowledge
or conscious effort,
whether we sleep or wake.

He follows his own
impulses only. Sometimes
we sleep, but he
is waking, and at other times
though we are waking
he cannot be aroused.
You may lead him to the water,
but he will not drink.
You may call him,
but he will not come until
good and ready.
Sometimes we desire
to use him—he refuses,

like an untrained dog
will not be brought to heel
or, coward-like, couches
with his tail between our legs.

Often he wants to act,
and it is we, authoritarian
or puritan, prohibit it.
He has a life, a personality,
a cast of features, and
an intelligence all
his own—and all
quite distinct from ours.
What a piece of work!
How express and admirable!
In action, how like an angel!

He is the victim and the scapegoat
of prurient segregation,
untouchable, discriminated against
like Negro, leper, homosexual—
all invisible men.
But he is no unperson. No—
in apprehension how like a god!
The beauty of the world!
The paragon of animals!

We are quite wrong
to be ashamed of naming him
and of displaying him.
Why should we always
seek to hide and cover
what we should show
and ornament and groom,
exhibit with all pomp and pride
as we do, less suitably,
the lesser members of
our grave anatomy?

Let us prove pricks and tools
are far from being fools!
Why should a good man hide
what may be his only joy and pride?
Let all our cocks be braved abroad
unto the glory of the Lord!

Amen.

TONGUE

Prick not the only
member without a bone.
I am its poor relation
but well above his
lowlier station.
I too can spit
hot spunky sparks
of love and wit, but only I
enjoy the taste of larks'
tongues and nightingales'
—though he likes humans' too,
in serpent kiss and slow
funnylingus or fellatio,
the fruitful suck.

Lap like a cat
the milk of words
and at the feast of Pentecost
with scarlet oriflammes
of fire and faith
speak with the tongues
of all men, all angels.

BELLY

Gut of my gut,
rumble thy hunger!
Humble the baron of beef,
unmake the wedding-cake!
Mumble approval
of Pekin duck
or angels on horseback,
pot-roast, pot-luck!

Breadbasket,
borborygmic bellybutton!
Big baywindow bauch!
Be flushed with wine
and dosed with paprika—
glutted be with grouse!

Murder the helpless
softboiled eggs,
dismember the tender rumps
of pretty babes,
and grind in your mills
all grist, in your jowls
all fish, flesh and fowls.

(Bow-wow! But hark!
I hear the ulcers bark!)

HEART

Surd despot,
apple core.
Beater about
the bony bush
of ribs and sternum,
captive word
of an imprisoned bird
who only seems

to sing, but longs
to fly away
into the open tree
of night and day—
small animal
worrying at the bars
of human cages
with quiet desperation
and sudden rages—
monster and machine
that pumps the dream
into attack,
but cannot realize
the perturbations of
its long distresses, or
the flexings
of its magic muscle—
always, always
tussling with itself
and overcoming
nothing but
its beatings,
beatings, beatings,
that are its wings
of love—the heart
and still the start
of all things, and
the stop.

ANGLES OF VISION

EXILE AND REINCARNATION

Perverse home-sickness, maritime nostalgia,
a longing to be anywhere but here,
willing self-banishment, into the back
of beyond, not just to 'someplace else'.

A thirst for the undrinkable
horizon, perpetual future, appetite
to touch untouchables, both
human and eternal.

A kind of early immortality, but still
with hope for an eventual rebirth, return
to the place from which one started—now,
fortunately, grown totally unrecognizable.

All those one thought one knew so well
or was indifferent to, thank goodness,
dead now; or gone away, intelligently,
as one had done oneself, long, long ago—

and who, even more intelligently,
have never come back.

Tashkent

LOST SOUL

on a picture taken in childhood

No camera can ever catch again
this visage, old before its time,
nor shutter the primeval rage
for solitude within
the absent social stance.

No tyrant power could exploit
that independence; no chemical expose
its tense invisibility, nor print
the cat's wary nonchalance
in an affected poise.

Even when as here, in early childhood,
vulnerable, yet
obscurely armoured in my undivided gaze—
a child alone, framed in a doorway:
a front of detestation in a scowl of pain.

*

Eyes lowering but straight,
brow big, mouth still unschooled in smiles,
a little Taurus, about to butt his horns
against a wrong already half-expected,
in a life already far too long.

The left fist clenched, in desperation,
as if for a battle he
knew in advance not worth the fight.
(One blue eye, the right,
already bruised and blackened.)

Baffled as an aborigine
afraid to lose, with the taking
of his likeness, an emergent soul:
a veiled yet penetrating frown
sunk in the sadness of primordial woe.

26

Wary of strangers' smiles,
suspicious of their ease, their looks,
of hands bearing gifts, caresses;
yet gulled with promises of beads,
baubles, toys broken as soon as touched.

Feeling himself no fool, but like a primitive
in love with all that was frivolous, shining:
unable to distinguish dream from life,
false from true, good from bad—
perhaps not wishing to.

*

I knew it from the start,
and see now how much wiser I was then:
I am all there, the essence
of the boy I cannot mask:
that child the father

of this man; that stocky dwarf
this delicate giant; that brave bull
this stricken deer; that dead David
this Jonathan—and this Goliath with the stone
embedded in his brow.

*

He sees it now: the pattern and
the picture of a life, a death—
something that did not have to be
but that a flash ordained as past and future
at a present age of three.

South Shields

THE SACRIFICE

at the grave of Yeats

Stone-hearted man,
in stones you lie,
dry in the spills of rain
under that stone-filled sky.

Under the stones of a carved cross
recording Cain
and Abel, the Fall of Man.
Each stone is pain.

Beneath your chiselled words,
beneath a cracked tower;
under the stone of a church
weighing each stony hour.

Under Maeve on Knocknarea,
Maeve the stony-still, alone—
under Ben Bulben's brow of rock—
bare bones, Old Rocky Face, bare stone.

*

Stone circles plunged in bramble pits,
the blaze of furze round blackened bogs,
sheep strewn like boulders on ferny hills,
the shores of rock, the mountain crags.

Ringed in a faery fort,
dungeoned by leaning slabs of cloud;
abbey altars ruined in rain,
drystone walls where bees are loud.

Stone is the heart, and stone the tongue,
stone is the harp, the dreamer's eye
shut in a stony sleep, with space
only for a passing sky.

Death too cold, and life too long.
(Time, dolmen of dew.)
Life too long, and love too bitter.
—Pass by. Nothing is true.

Drumcliff

IN MEMORIAM: BERTRAND RUSSELL

In another February, on a Sunday afternoon eight years ago,
I wept for you, and for a world that could reject your voice.

You were so frail, so ancient; yet stronger than us all.
You stood beside me on a platform in Trafalgar Square
among the toothless lions of a tyrannous imperial pride,
under the shadow of Nelson strutting in the falling snow.

Your head was bare, and your wild white hair
blazed like your mind in the wind of whirling flakes.
Your face, the mask of a tragic hawk,
was sad and bitter as you cried your warnings and defiance
at the armed forces of error, the police of Britain,
the criminal politicians, the priests of power, the insane
manufacturers of arms and poison gas and atom bombs,
inhuman profiteers all, sucking the blood of human misery.

You stood alone before the gathered heads of microphones,
tilted intelligently, raised like vipers, cobras about to strike.
—But like a saint, or like Apollo, god of poetry and music,
you charmed them into peace. You won their love with love,
with the fearless beauty of your mind, your noble voice.

Dear man, I remember your friendship for the lost and helpless,
and the grasp of your withered hand in mine that February day,
delicate but strong. I remember the wise humour of your smile,
twisted yet pure; the sparkle in your hooded, sombre eyes;
the deep lines in your cheeks; the nose like a mountain peak.
—And O, that great and simple brow—so vast, so calm, so full!

Most of all, I remember how you taught me to have courage
to defy the world in solitude; how to disarm
the dangerous stupidity of man, using weapons not of this world—
intellect with love; wit with pity; candour with compassion.

Now, in a foreign snow, my tears are falling for you,
and for the world, that did not heed your warning cries.

Tokyo, February 3rd 1970

EMILY IN WINTER

Born in December, from the start
You knew a sunstruck winter of the heart.

Gales now blow clouds of snowdust ghosts, that bloom
with rainbows round your black-railed room.

I come once more with flowers and alone
to speak with you behind your stone.

You who can move upon the crusted whitenesses
and leave no track; I press

my handprint on the snow, and feel the heat
above the buried breastbone where your heart once beat.

Amherst

NOSTALGIE DE LA BOUE

The gutter lies around me where I fall—
the grit, rags, litter, filth and spit
of life that has no meaning in its gall,
and drags its madness through a waste of shit.

There are no dead leaves any more,
only the paper shells of self and lust;
returning to the grave whose worms I bore,
I eat myself, my mouth is chocked with dust.

I am my own deep, stinking pit of blood,
my own self-coffiner and rancid priest.
I look with unshut eyes upon a world of mud.
I am the last, the lowest and the least.

Kuala Lumpur

ANNUNCIATION

Tilted, the unreflecting glass
throws on its back
one corner of the room.

In a vase, a long lily,
out of true, does not falter.
A marble does not roll.

The spirit level
still centres its bead
of air. Out of plumb,

the abandoned body of
the floorboards is outflung,
parallels of dust converging on

infinity, a mousehole.
Those deranged bedclothes,
old snows of crumpled news.

Overhead, a slanted window
stabs her with shaft on shaft of sun,
leans its lightweight hard on her—

angel of glass whose pinions,
still billowing with the winds of flight,
are checked curtains signalling

like rally flags
news of a triumph to
devastated streets.

ECONOMIC ANIMAL FARM

TOKI

'The Bird of Time has but a little way
To fly—and Lo! the Bird is on the Wing . . .'
(*Rubáiyát of Omar Khayyám*, FitzGerald translation)

O rare bird, red heron,
scarlet crested ibis, you
native of Eastern Asia,
once the subject of poems,
paintings, fans and screens
in China, Japan, Korea—
but now a dying breed.

In China and Korea
your heron's crested head, tinged
on the cheeks and bill with red and orange,
no longer graces ricefields.
Your white, slender body like a vase
no longer stands among the green rice-shoots.
Your vermilion shanks and feet
no longer wade the paddy pools.
Your pink-lined wings
flash no more across the bamboo glades.

No poet celebrates you now.
No painter spreads your pinions
on the gold-squared sky of screens,
or lets your beak dip
among the sticks of a white fan.

No poet celebrates you now.
How can you be a harbinger of luck,
when your own has been so bad?
—So I shall celebrate you now
in this poem that is your funeral ode.

'For these dead birds sigh a prayer. . . .'

*

Once, twelve of you survived.
Japan was your final home,
your nests of snow
on Sado Island's Mount Kokuryu,
on northern winter's
remote peninsula of Noto.

There I saw you once—
a single bird
silently flying the lonely sky
above the cliffs of snow.
Yes, that was where men saw you last.

In the first year of Meiji, 1868,
Japan became 'Westernized',
and it was decreed, as one of the first
steps towards equality (illusion
of every new society), that hunting
might be indulged in by the general public.

Against the tenets of Buddha, it was then
the slaughter of the birds and beasts began
in deadly earnest. A long, slow,
ritual assassination.
Advancing from feudalism, Japan
stepped back into the darkest
pit of barbarism. This was decreed.

*

Today, Japan is flourishing.
But we must consider her in a decline
when her wild birds are killed
by thoughtless hunters.

The Japanese economy is booming.
But you, rare birds, are dying, murdered
by polluted streams and poisoned fields,
the rich waste of industry.

Dying, you became a legend,
creating in your death the mystery and
immortality of the Arabian bird,
the phoenix, fabulous image of eternity.
—For death is now the *toki*'s nest. . . .

Yes, your song is becoming a legend,
like your life, your death.
What are the Japanese becoming?
By their own admission, a race
of mere 'economic animals'.

*

Now it is reported
that even those last twelve
have not been seen again
on Sado Island's Mount Kokuryu,
on northern winter's
remote peninsula of Noto.

Were you killed by black Siberian kites,
by hawks, or by the icy storms of Sado's seas?

No. You were killed by our neglect.
Through our indifference and greed
a beauty has gone from these islands.
A mystery, too,
never to return.

*

Japan is losing all mystery.
Having become prosperous, bourgeois,
she has also become boring.

It is not you, *toki*, but man
the destroyer who should be destroyed.
You, a bird of cleanly habits,
a delicate eater, were destroyed
by man, who fouls his own nest,
a nest of atomic dust and ashes.

39

In time, *toki*, in time
even your legendary memory will die.
Then beauty will be dead indeed,
and mystery and poetry too.
There will be no more birds and poets—all
killed by our hands of iron,
our hearts of stone.

'The bird of wonder dies. . . .'
Unlike the phoenix,
we cannot rise again
from our nest of ashes, nest of snows.

LOST DOG

Endlessly trotting,
stopping a second.
not to sniff, but
to look—down a lane,
into faces that ignore you,
trotting on again
with that exhausted
inexhaustibility.
You are lost, and know it.

Dogs with homes and owners
stand and watch you
trotting in mad traffic.
They do not speak to you.
They do not help you.
In Japan, anyone who
does not belong is suspect.
You are an outcast.
You are lost, and know it.

Panting, pink tongue hanging
loose from jaws parted
in a frightened smile,
sharp ears cocked for
the voice of a man who once
called you by name,
tail endlessly wagging
when children stop you.
You are lost, and they know it.

But children are no good.
You know it. They
are not masters.
They pet your impatience
with clumsy gaiety.

Grateful for the least touch
of humanity, of warmth,
you have no spirit
to bite their cruel fingers.

A tramp in the park
attaches himself to you,
but you feel somehow
it's no good—you are off
endlessly trotting, up steps,
down lanes, across highways,
through the grounds of shrines;
trying to look normal, you
conceal desperation everyone sees.

Everyone sees you are lost,
and turns away from you.
Where is your famed
Japanese sense of direction?
Can't you smell your way
home, like a cat? No,
you're not that clever.
Tokyo: demented maze of
lights and indifference.

Night fell long ago, but still
you trot, endlessly trot. In Tokyo,
the world's biggest, but
not greatest, city there are
so many streets, so few
homes for the lost, the sad,
the desperate, the abandoned.
In your situation, a man
would commit suicide.

A face, a voice, a stroking hand
that you will never know again—
these are the memories you run to.

Scraps in the gutters disgust you:
your drink the water scattered
in front of shops to lay the dust.
Why have you no collar,
no name, no address?
Yes, you have a name. Taro.

But you can't tell it to anyone.
Besides, nearly every dog
is called Taro in Japan.
It is a voice, not a name
you answer to. An accent.
When I call 'Taro!' you
stop a second, wild with hope.
But the voice isn't right.
Who wants a foreigner, anyway?

What was your master's name?
Your eyes are filled with
dumb information, the long
history of a dog's life.
Kicks, blows, fights, bruises,
cuts, whippings, houndings by
cats, trucks, children, cars.
Patient waitings for masters,
scraps of dirty rice.

Now your movie
flickers its last reel.
The fire-engines
howl, but not for you;
ambulances scream,
but not for you; mobile
blood-transfusion units wail,
but not for you.
You are still lost, and know it.

The policeman halts traffic,
but not for you; signals change,
doors open, but not for you;
cherry blooms, but not for you;
children wave bye-bye,
but not for you.
Night falls. Night falls.
But not for you.
You are still lost, and know it.

Endlessly trotting,
you pant through the city
of empty neon. No one
in the streets. You run
down the middle of roads,
your feathery tail
waving wildly in headlamps
of prowling taxis.
You are lost forever, and you know it.

Endlessly trotting into
the dawn of a new day.
But dawn is only
chill neon, not the sun.
You trot endlessly on, knowing
this is your last day, knowing
this is your last light, knowing
this is your last breath, knowing
they know you are lost, they know you are lost.

VISITING THE GRAVES IN ZOSHIGAYA CEMETERY

to Takeyoshi

It is a fine Sunday morning,
an autumn in December.

Here, in hard and stony Tokyo
there is a place of peace and gentleness.
There are trees and bushes
that cast moving leaf-shadows
over memorial stones
and tablets in which the shadowed names
are deeply cut by winter sun.

At the gardener's cottage
one can borrow a simple home-made broom—
bamboo twigs of *mosodake*—
and an old water-bucket made of faded wood
in which a water-ladle
leans like an everlasting flower.

It is like a small city here.
The stone monuments and steps and little walls
are like houses, villas, castles for souls.

But it is a city of silence.
There are only gardeners in its streets,
and birds.
Joined now by
the shadows of our shades.

Here and there are white posts
and signboards on which black characters
are barely brushed.
They point in the direction of
the graves we are to visit.

45

The paths of earth
that a long night frosted
begin to thaw, but
they are fringed still with ice.

Here is the grave
of Koizumi Yakumo.
A few withered flowers
stand in the stone holders.
We put fresh water in,
and a few new flowers—red
chrysanthemums, and yellow,
and a few small narcissi.

With the broom
we sweep your grave, and tidy the weeds.

Then we light a small bonfire
of dead maple leaves and
the paper wrappings from
bundles of dark-green incense sticks,
which we kindle in the flames
and place before your stone,
the stone of your wife,
the stone of your family—
three stones that are more than stone.

These stones are severe and calm,
but they are not hard like the streets of Tokyo.
They are surrounded by trees and plants—
dwarf azaleas, a Chinese pine,
a jasmine or a gardenia,
a large shady tree, and a hedge
of spindle bushes within
a low bamboo fence.

The stones live among the leaves'
shifting shadows, and
seem to move a little
when a faint breeze stirs the branches.

For these are not just stones.
They are the memories of men.
Lafcadio Hearn, this morning
I came to speak to you,
and saw the sun
cast shadows of
your name's sharp-edged characters
(Koizumi Yakumo)
into their calligraphic canyons,
and saw the sharp edges
of your name in Japanese—
four noble characters—
cast deep shadows into their own
sunny pits.
One day I hope to see them brushed
with flakes, drifted with snow.

A nearby level-crossing
sounds your only bell.

*

By the grave of Yumeji Takehisa,
he who drew women like no one else,
there was a large, bare zelkova tree
in which a long-tailed bird
perched and sang in the winter light.

Your stone is small and modest,
your name engraved in white
on the black slab sparkling with mica,
like a night sky with stars.

*

Here are the stones of actors—
Onoe Baiko, Ichimura Hazaemon—
and of a dramatist, Shimamura Hogetsu.
There the graves of other writers—
Natsumi Soseki, Kafu Nagai.

Near them is the tall stone
of Naruse Jinzo, a great man,
a great teacher, in whose house
I now live.

I come to give him
my greetings, and to announce
my residence in his house.

And to thank him
for his hospitality to a stranger.

*

In one lane of the cemetery
three young ladies
were playing battledore and shuttlecock.
The sunlight blazed
through the shuttlecock's white feathers
as it raced across the sky,
pursued by an enormous crow.
And at last,
as we left the cemetery,
we passed, like spirits,
through the smoke of a gatekeeper's bonfire.

EXPOEM

We land on a new moon now, man-made. To enter these gates of sun
is to take one first and giant step into adventure, the unknown,
into the future of mankind. On moving walkways, on clouds of glass
and steel, our feet are light, though not with weightlessness.

Here are no craters, moondust or rocks of sinister shape.
This moon has trashboxes, toilets, hotdogs, sushi, movies, carparks.
On this human scale, man cannot feel too lost or helplessly small,
but rather, comfortably at home in fantasy, fact or fun.

In palaces of light, caves of invention, towers of the sun,
in fairs of flowers, magic gardens, under ballooning tents of roofs,
we hear—in hope, not fear—the harmonies of time and space,
and meet our fellow-men with gifts and smiles, not politics and
    bombs.

And remember always, amid the wonder and delight, our cosmonaut,
our ordinary hero, the workman whose patience, craft and strength
    created
this outpost of the stars. Under his helmet—white or green or
    yellow—
he trod before us every inch of this new moon. And came bringing
    peace.

DEATH OF A JAPANESE ESPERANTIST

in memory of Tadanoshin Yui

Outside Prime Minister Sato's official residence
you, Tadanoshin Yui, an old scholar
and a lifelong student of Esperanto,
kneeled down, but not in prayer.

It was a cold day, but clear. November.
You kept your old overcoat on,
though it was not to keep you warm.
There was a deeper flame.

Your old suit and overcoat
were drenched in icy gasoline.
Looking for the green star of hope,
you struck your last match.

You left behind you this pure
statement of your intentions:
'I am fully aware that it is useless for
a mere citizen like myself to appeal to the government. . . .'

Such is democracy. Your act was pure,
but useless. The wars continue.
Okinawa will not be returned just yet.
Japan protests with violence, not peace.

Your suicide was gentle in its peace,
its humble indignation. Let us remember
your peace, before we strike the final match
of mad mass-destruction by nuclear bombs!

You, at least, old man,
were sane. We cannot say as much of ourselves,
or of our world, our self-appointed leaders.
My verdict on you: death of sound mind.

SHOJI

Both door
and window,
screen and
illumination,
paper cell
of light,
sliding wall
of flakes on
shell of sun.

Both frame
and fence,
open book
inscribed by
nothing, or
only the rain's
fingers, moths,
sootfalls, ghosts'
aerial brushings.

Glass without
reflection glazed.
Calm hive, pale
drum, bare cloud.
A season's lake,
pure white sail
or cool shroud
lit with a moment's
moving shade—

Blossoms, boughs,
water flowing,
birds flying,
leaves falling,
moon rising,
lantern lighting—
translucent
fan of summer,
fall, winter, spring.

Ice-fringed,
deep-grassed,
fluttered by gale
of stone, or
dusty butterfly:
frail shadows
of heads, hands—
the perforations of
dawn, stars, eyes.

HEART MURMURS

PROMISES

'Take this kiss upon the brow . . .' (Edgar Allan Poe)

We plighted our troth
after the fashion of
those too poor for rings.
She painted the nail
of my lefthand little finger
with her metallic, dark green
nail varnish, sealed
with a fingerprint before it dried.

I kissed her long
below the left breast,
leaving an exclamation
that in a day had turned
to black and blue, a bruise
shaped like my smile,
a promise or a warning.
Such was our betrothal.

But such plain tokens of affection
last no longer than rings or vows.
Soon that smile faded,
on her breast and in my heart.
We parted on Canal Street
promising never to meet again.
On Bourbon Street, the bars
were bright with funeral jazz.

Now the mark has left her heart.
That breast is white with time again.
But on my lefthand little finger
the nail grows slowly, never grows out.
Though a pale half-moon now appears below,
the old varnish lingers, stained and dull
like a hurt quick, hit by the hammer of love
and long in going, long in going.

Though I have kept my promise,
she broke that word of honour
to always live alone, to live
the dream within the dream.
—There is no logic in our lot.
She in her wisdom has remembered
the promise of that kiss upon the heart:
and I in my folly have forgot.

New Orleans

THREE SINGERS

I. *Nina Simone at the 'Village Gate'*

Face of a brainy,
precocious child—
'The Times Are Changing'
'It's the Morning of My Life'
then 'Turning Point'—a very
touching little tale
of little white girl and her
little black schoolfriend,
last line is 'Oh, I see. . . '.
Just great.

'I'm Gonna Leave You.'
She has the air
of a princess, a
Benin bronze. Poem by
Paul Laurence Dunbar
as a song, 'Compensation'
('An' if you dunno
who Dunbar was, find out.')
'God in his great compassion
gave me the gift of soul. . . .'

The way she turns
while playing and
peers through the spots
at me over her
slight left shoulder,
hunch of a hunch.
'Someone out there,'
she mutters, not
seeing I see her.

'Any Day Now I Shall Be Released.'
No smiles, few words,

scornful; only gesture
a lifting, very occasional,
of right hand and forefinger.
Revival revivalism.

'I Ain't Got No One'
(terrific). Sometimes
half-rises to sing a phrase
into the pendant mike
angled over the Steinway
that seems hardly able to believe
her fingers, her voice.
—'I Could Eat a Book.'
What a joy to be alive
in the same room as Nina. . . .

'I Put a Spell on You.'

*

II. *Anita O'Day at 'The Half Note'*

Hookey's and the 5-Spot all closed down,
only the Half Note now,
corner Spring and Hudson,
going since 1957, one
of the oldest in the Village.

Roy Eldridge warming up
(he's still wearing his glasses—
he takes them off to get hot).
Plays and sings
'Have You Ever Loved a Woman?'
'Everything you do is wrong—
like Hong Kong.'
Private fun in the band—Roy's
lovely mischievous grin.
Snub Mosley on slide trombone
'and slide sax'.

It's Anita!
She's really here!
Neat in white lace
(from Bangkok, she told me later,
'Just did a Far East tour there,
not Japan, though—they're nuts'.
She makes all her own dresses—
there's a girl for you!)

Unbelievable.
Her first number, for me alone,
'Let Me Off Uptown'.
(Shall I ever forget?)
'Yesterday.'
'Try Your Wings.'
'Do You Know the Way to San José?'—
just great! She shreds a lyric like e. e. cummings.

Those little white gloves
caress the mike. She smiles
softly (that brown mole
upper lip left of centre),
waves at my strobe flash,
'They Can't Take that Away from Me',
'Let's Fall in Love',
I'm not going to cry any more—
'Let Someone Start Believing in You—
Watch what Happens . . .'.

She signs me a record even she
has forgotten, it's so rare—
EP Norgran 'Anita Sings' and she writes
'To James—and one of our most
treasured possessions—from
Anita O'Day'.
Next set: she says, 'Change the pace a little bit'—
her favourite phrase. And mine.

*

III. *Ode to a Favourite Jazz Singer*

Our Ella,
sweetheart in heaven,
hollered be thy name.

Thy swingdom drum,
thy thrill be fun
in Perth as it is in Harlem.

Live up in play
our daily dead.

Unfasten our best dresses
as we unfasten them
that undress against us.

But deliver us from evil
and from the boll-weevil.

For thine is the swingdom,
the only pretty ringdom.

For thine is the kingdom
and the flower—
and the ghost of Kid Ory—

O Ella,
our Ella—
yea, men!

EPSTEIN'S 'LAZARUS'

Head turned backwards, you review
the dark from which you came—
hands, fingers fluttering faint and free
as forest-captured birds within the swathing
boughs and branches of your loosened cerements.

Pale, too. Haunted by that single night's
acquaintance with the dead. Recreated from the black
tomb of stone by light's chill resurrection, an apprentice
apparition, early-risen, suddenly bestir yourself, return
a past master among these ever-present ghosts.

Jesus has gone. Now your lost companions rejoin you.
Though once, in sickness and in death,
you were even more remote, less one of us,
another kind of strangeness, a distance
divide you from us now.

Friends, brothers, lovers, animals, all
come to welcome you on your return. But it is not
as if you entered from some ordinary voyaging.
More than after the sailor's year-long separations
these lost loved ones curiously look into your eyes—

and deep below their smiles and sweet embraces
you feel the horror hidden in these wondering faces.

DORIAN GRAY TRIES OUT THE LATEST
POLAROID MODEL

Rip off each revelation as it comes!
Brave the technicolor of a butchershop
or grainy black and white—no
merciful sepia softness here—and see
stark noon turn into starker night
within one instamatic tear.

That face that lunched upon a thousand lips
in love, lust, lechery and 'just for a lark'
now darkens in the window of a grave,
the eyes grown sombre—still
with a spark of their incorrigible laughter, but
lost now forever in the skull's unending cave.

EXPRESS ELEVATOR

Stillstand
and fly
upon a
highspeed
sigh.

Liftoff
is straight
as die
re-entry
dragging fate.

Stops
remind me
of the man
I left
behind me.

Snatched
into hope
the wrong
end of this
telescope.

Plunged
into deep
grief, the far
start of this
telesleep.

The shaft
is brown
the count
up is
also down.

The body
soars
express
and lighted
ninety floors.

Heart sunk
in sand
soul sucked
down miles
of wind.

Up from
helltops
angel into
heaven
drops.

New York: Empire State Building

THE ROWER

Unendingly, against a broad stream strained, my oars,
Alas, detach me from the smiling countryside.
O soul, with oars your heavy hands are loaded,
And now the slow waves' knell must take the place of skies.

With hard heart, and blind to the beauties I destroy,
While round me the circular ripples are unfurled,
I will, with mighty strokes, dissolve the lustrous world
Of leaves and fire that I sing of quietly.

The trees' smooth-mirrored amplitude on which I float—
Waters, painted with boughs and leaves, that faultless stand—
Rend, rend them all, my bark, inflict on them a wound
That will obliterate their vast remembered quiet.

Never, enchanted day, never has your beauty
Suffered at rebel hands such lawless violence;
But now, my life, as in my sun-drawn childhood, turns
To the source where even names, and all things, cease to be.

In vain the nymph opposes her enormous length,
Impedes my weary body with a pure embrace—
I gradually break a thousand bonds of ice,
Her whole silvery-bearded body's naked strength.

This river's stealthy-sounding waters curiously
Blind my golden daytime with a silken bandage:
Nothing can dull more pitilessly joy's keen edge
Than Time's wings beating with observed monotony.

Under the looped bridges the deep wave bears me on,
Through caverns filled with the wind's murmuring darkness.
They flow upon a brow weighed down with weariness:
But sterner than their admissions is its proud bone.

Their night is long. Behind them the soul imprisons
Its sensitive suns beneath unfailing eyelids—
Then, with a movement clothing me in stones, downwards
I glide, scorning such deep, deep azure indolence.

(From the French of Paul Valéry)

THE MAGI

Balthazar, Melchior and Caspar, the three Wise Kings,
Bearing chalices of silver, gold, and rare enamels,
And attended by a caravan of nine white camels,
Proceed like figures out of old illuminings.

From distant Orient they carry precious things
In homage to God's only son, born that all evils
Be forgiven here below, in men and animals.
A black page bears their trains of gold embroiderings.

To the door of the manger, where Saint Joseph stands,
They reverently come, with their crowns in their hands,
To greet the Holy Child who smiles at their splendour.

In the imperial reign of Augustus Caesar
Thus they came, bearing gold, and frankincense, and myrrh,
The three Wise Kings—Caspar, Melchior and Balthazar.

(From the French of José Maria de Hérédia)

THREE CATS

I. *Mouser*

The cat, black-masked, trots with level back
  and tail slung low
along the glass-fanged village wall;
    breaks quietly
his clockwork's easygoing flow
    and stops,
one slim white paw in-curled, and ears
    askance,
his pale eyes wide, alight,
    yet not quite
understanding us as he stares down.

Then just as easygoingly runs on,
a busy cat, who has no use
for idle men who call 'Puss-puss!'

II. *Cosy Cat Nap*

Pussy-kitten, pussy-cat,
purring on the kitchen-mat,
how I like your furry tail
curl'd around you like a snail.

Pussy-kitten, pussy-cat,
purring on the kitchen mat;
fire tinkles in the grate,
clocks tick tip-toe, very late.

Pussy-kitten, pussy-cat,
purring on the kitchen mat;
hear the iron softly stamp
on steaming washing, warm and damp.

Pussy-kitten, pussy-cat,
purring on the kitchen mat;
squeeze your eyes right out of sight,
and doze and blink and doze all night!

Pussy-kitten, pussy-cat,
purring on the kitchen mat;
purroo, purroo,
purroo, purroo. . . .

Pussy-kitten, pussy-cat,
purrooing on the kitchen mat.

III. *Black Tom*

A black cat in a green and sunny field,
ears peaked—one slender, lifted paw—
points like a dog his quivering tail,
whiskers bristling in knife-edge grasses.

What do his pale eyes impale? A shrew?
A bumbling bee, or those two butterflies,
weaving the nettles, that seem to tumble
under-over one another in the lazy air?

His pale eyes, burning bright, his glossy fur
to me will always be as new, the field as green;
and always blue the passing sky of that late summer day.
—But never will he move. And never seize his unknown prey.

Wensleydale